Harmensz van Rijn Rembrandt

Layout: Baseline Co. Ltd.
127-129A Nguyen Hue
Fiditourist Building, 3rd Floor
District 1, Ho Chi Minh City,
Vietnam.

ISBN: 978-1-904310-81-5

Printed in China

Harmensz van Rijn Rembrandt

sirrocco

In the days when Dutch merchants traded in the Far East and the Antipodes, a miller named Harmen Gerritszoon van Rijn lived in Leyden. He had eyes only for the son who was born on 15 July, 1606, at the start of a century which promised so much and was so auspicious for men of destiny.

The child was later to be known simply as Rembrandt, his first Christian name. The young Rembrandt soon manifested the artistic skills, which his teachers discerned from his earliest years. After studying the humanities in his home town, the young boy who had not yet passed his fourteenth birthday, enrolled at the university claiming to be an accomplished draughtsman.

In 1621, Rembrandt became the pupil of Jacob van Swanenburgh, and completed his studies in the studio of Pieter Lastman, whose paintings of large frescoes of historical scenes instilled in him a love of precision, detail and sumptuous backgrounds of the type in which his master excelled. Rembrandt's official apprenticeship was relatively short. In 1625, the young Rembrandt set himself up in his own studio, ready to fulfil his own ambitions by trying his wings like other young men of his generation whom trade with India had precipitated into a different adventure, seeking to make their fortune. All Rembrandt had were his pencils with which he hoped to earn the comfortable living of which he dreamed and which his father, who died in 1630, had been lucky enough to see emerge from the tip of the paintbrush.

Whilst still studying under Lastman, Rembrandt painted many scenes from the Bible in which certain objects were illuminated with a conventional spirituality, which was often unusual but sincere from a pictorial point of view. He was inspired not so much by mysticism but the special mystery of the biblical story. Details such as the fabric of a headdress or the shadow of a column emerging from the background were highlighted to give emphasis. The painter's own faith made him able to translate the saintliness of the figures to the canvas.

Rembrandt was no longer sacrificing the subject-matter to the theatricality of the masters of his day, Caravaggio and Manfredi, whose work he found trivial. Rembrandt, at the age of twenty, was not the artistic heir of Michelangelo and the mannerists. When he lost himself in the excitement of painting, he was neither consciously a realist nor an expressionist. He merely listened to his inner voice and

1. *Self-Portrait with Lace Collar*, c. 1629. Oil on canvas, 37.7 x 28.9 cm. Mauritshuis, The Hague.

5

created an atmosphere of magic which he alone experienced but which he was able to convey in his paintings through the use of light and line.

To understand this inner emotion is to enter into what a critic would later call Rembrandt's "tragic expression", which as early as 1626 was already perceptible in the most famous paintings now in the Pushkin Museum in Moscow, such as *Christ Driving the Money-Changers from the Temple*. The clear, bright colour scheme of this biblical panel bears the hallmark of Pieter Lastman, yet despite a certain lack of harmony and unity, imperfect anatomy and doubtful perspective, the painting has an inner glow, a sort of premonition of the painter's genius and a strength of feeling which is greater than in his later works, when his technique had improved so extensively but his excitement and enthusiasm were no longer at their peak.

Human emotions and the passions of the soul occupied pride of place in seventeenth-century philosophy. These were transmuted to canvas by painters, and was spoken of in the salons of the day. When the young Rembrandt depicted the wrath of the young Christ and the shocked money-changers shaken out of their routine, he was exploring the matters which preoccupied his contemporaries. The artist's intention was not to distance himself from philosophical debate, he was posing the problem in pictorial terms which contained in themselves his intellectual emancipation and the stamp of his unique artistic approach.

Rembrandt's work showed none of the abstract and rather stilted "passions" of Lastman and his contemporaries. He patiently constructed his vision of the world and its inhabitants using a powerful natural and evocative touch. In later years, his spiritual nature and his artistic technique would produce an "aesthetic of emotion" without parallel.

He perfectly controlled light and space in his paintings. His credo was to work from life, and he adhered to this throughout his life. It was at this same period that the young painter began to make prints and produced a series of striking little portraits of himself.

2. The Anatomy Lesson by Dr. Tulp, 1632.
Oil on canvas,
169.5 x 216.5 cm.
Mauritshuis, The Hague.

These faces, sometimes grimacing sometimes wearing a sardonic or iron expression, are always very expressive. They provide a foretaste of the portraits he would paint from the 1630s onwards. There are no self-portraits in the Russian museums, whose

collections form the main subject of this book, but the portraits in the Hermitage in St Petersburg and the Pushkin Museum in Moscow, entitled *Portrait of an Old Man* and painted in 1631, are examples of his earliest commissions which made his reputation as well as being the foundations of his wealth. As soon as his fortunes improved, he began to climb the social ladder as his parents had so fervently hoped.

3. *The Company of Frans Banning Cocq and Willem Van Ruytenburch* also known as *The Night Watch*, 1642. Oil on canvas, 363 x 437 cm. Rijksmuseum, Amsterdam.

He was only 22 years old when he took his first pupil into his studio. He had not yet mastered all the skills he needed from his teachers and his "imitations" of Lastman lacked assurance, but even if he was still "timid" in comparison with his later work, he never relented to convention.

The infinite milling crowds of juxtaposed figures still eluded him, he was lost in a host of isolated subtleties; but he had already convinced several of his contemporaries that he was indeed skilled, and they were responsible for his gaining a reputation. Constantyn Huygens, secretary to Prince Frederick Henry, a poet and traveller of refined tastes did not hesitate to compare him to Jan Lievens, who exhibited unparalleled precociousness in the quality of his youthful work. On 20 June, 1631, an Antwerp art dealer, Hendrijk van Uylengurgh, signed a contract with the young Rembrandt, offering to set him up in his house in Amsterdam.

4. *Lazarus' Resurrection,*
   1630-1631.
   The British Museum,
   London.

The *Portrait of an Old Man* shows great originality in the choice of size and other inherent aspects of the picture. A painting's effect depends on its size and the distance which separates it from the viewer. In this work, Rembrandt lends space to his composition. The painterly devices he uses are diverse and his brushstrokes, sometimes discreet, sometimes more noticeable, translate the expressiveness of the model, by revealing his feelings as well as his features and social standing. Rembrandt's experience of the "passions of the soul" breathes life into what would merely have been a two-dimensional portrait had it been painted by another artist of his generation.

The *Anatomy Lesson by Dr Tulp*, painted in 1832, was commissioned by the Amsterdam Guild of Surgeons, as a result of the *Portrait*, whose owner had quickly spread his enthusiasm for the painter. Rembrandt was young and proud and hardly ever left the studio. The *Self-Portrait in a Cap* in the Cassel Museum, painted in 1634, shows him very much in command of himself, strong and confident of his future. He knew how to vary his compositions depending on the model, yet at the same time he was

5. *The Descent from the Cross*, 1633. Etching.

6. *Self-Portrait at the Age of Thirty-Four*, 1639-1640. Oil on canvas, 102 x 80 cm. The National Gallery, London.

constantly satisfying the demands of a permanent apprenticeship which enabled him to improve his technique and methods with each canvas he painted. This can be seen in *Young Man in a Lace Collar*, now in the Hermitage Museum in St Petersburg. This portrait, which was painted in 1634, meets the standards of the time, but already reveals a ghostly and unconventional understanding in the facial expression, in which the relaxed manner of the sitter emphasises his pleasant smile and the lightness of his features. The chiaroscuro gives the whole picture a sense of reality of tone which may well have flattered the young dandy who was concerned to look well turned-out, and one can feel the strength of the life spark which the artist captured for posterity.

It was during this decade that Rembrandt firmly established his reputation. While continuing to produce the same kind of portraits as his contemporaries, he constantly produced illustrations for contemporary writings and mythology through a succession of paintings in which his imagination was allowed a free rein. While at the height of his technical skills, the painter decided to place his models in a context. They were often submerged in scenery full of historical allusions, appearing in costume or surrounded by carefully-worked symbols. Despite this fancy dress, the men and women portrayed revealed their personalities without ever sacrificing the originality of the genre.

Rembrandt married Saskia van Uylenburgh on 10 July, 1634 and she posed for him in the first year of their marriage. During this era he also produced a few grisaille paintings as curiosities. The *Adoration of the Magi*, painted in 1632, is one of these less happy experiments, much practised by his contemporaries, but extremely rare in Rembrandt's work. He used one or two of these experimental works as originals from which to make etchings, but these were limited to a few test-pieces which he found sufficiently unsatisfactory to cause him to abandon this line of endeavour.

There are few sketches by Rembrandt, apart from those which have now been revealed by taking x-rays of a few of his paintings. These do not enable us to establish the exact genesis of his paintings, but by comparing them with the grisailles he has left us, one can get a fair idea of the manner in which he painted. The only colours on his palette would be white, ochre and lamp black, and he would cover the canvas with large patches of transparent sepia which almost always remained intact where shade was called for in the painting; then the lit parts of the faces were modelled by a trace of white which would be worked in the shaded areas in long black or brown strokes. This is how the *Adoration of the Magi* was composed, though there were

7. *Christ Driving the Money-Changers from the Temple,* 1635. Etching.

8. *Christ Driving the Money-*
   Changers from the Temple,
   1626. Oil on wood panel
   (oak), 43.1 x 32 cm.
   The Pushkin Museum
   of Fine Arts, Moscow.

9. *Portrait of a Scholar*,
   1631. Oil on canvas,
   104.5 x 92 cm.
   The State Hermitage
   Museum, St Petersburg.

numerous retouchings, repaintings and constant modifications until the work was deemed to be completed. Through this analysis, it can be seen that ten years later, in *The Money-Changers in the Temple*, the artist had lost nothing of his fiery temperament, but on the other hand, being less subject to getting carried away, he was in fuller control of the subject-matter.

10. *The Adoration of the Magi*, 1632. Drawing. Kupferstichkabinett, Berlin.

It was during these years that he created a series of paintings on biblical themes, one of which, *The Incredulity of St Thomas* (1634) is in Moscow and three others – *The Descent from the Cross* (1634), *Abraham's Sacrifice* (1635) and *The Parable of the Labourers in the Vineyard* (1637) – are in St Petersburg.

11. *The Adoration of the Magi,*
1632.
Oil on paper pasted on
canvas, 45 x 39 cm.
The State Hermitage
Museum, St Petersburg.

12. *John the Baptist Preaching*,
   1634–1635.
   Oil on canvas,
   62.7 x 82.1 cm.
   Gemäldegalerie, Berlin.

Rembrandt's imagination dictated the settings, which were always very theatrical and particularly "lively". Life, as depicted by Rembrandt, was translated by a very powerful mimicry and his desire to confront history and those who made it, and to "dramatise" these events in order to render them "truer" and more convincing.

Under his brush, the theology of the event he is depicting becomes "humanised" by the setting, the dress and the light. In fact the artist's approach was one which the Reformation had created in artistic interpretation.

The Protestants took Holy Writ as a subject for historical and philosophical study, and considered biblical texts as a genuine source of historical material, rather than a series of parables and images. Almost from the outset, a strong tendency appeared in Protestant art to reproduce not merely the symbolic, but the literal meaning of biblical

14. *Portrait of a Boy.*
Oil on wood (oak),
67 x 47.5 cm.
The State Hermitage
Museum, St Petersburg.

15. *Portrait of a Young
    Woman with Flowers in
    Her Hair*, 1634.
    National Gallery of
    Scotland, Edinburgh.

16. *Young Man with
    a Lace Collar*, 1634.
    Oil on wood panel (oak),
    70.5 x 52 cm, oval.
    The State Hermitage
    Museum, St Petersburg.

17. *Rembrandt and Saskia*,
   1636.
   The Pierpont Morgan
   Library, New York.

18. *Flora*, 1634.
   Oil on canvas,
   125 x 201 cm.
   The State Hermitage
   Museum, St Petersburg.

stories too. Rembrandt was very taken with this intellectual approach and from the late 1620s, depicted several important scenes in order to demythologise them. This prosaic interpretation of the Bible was not unique to Rembrandt, but more than any other artist, he was able to give them an incomparable internal strength.

Rembrandt's artistic vision also betrays close ties to the Dutch tradition of painting. Yet he strongly dissociated himself from the concept of History behind the host of paintings created at the time which he considered to be impersonal and lacking in the "imagination" which, in his opinion, would have brought them to life.

He is thus close to represent a very "oriental" world as the thread linking his "scenes". Yet this decade is characterised equally by a change in his method of painting, which is an analysis of his *Danae*, of which the first version was painted in 1636, but which

was completely reworked ten years later, makes it easier to understand. This painting clearly exposes the artist's interior world at a moment when it was fast evolving and reveals the "spirit" of his ambitions. Between the two dates, Rembrandt's art had undergone radical changes. *Danae*, when studied in its two different versions, shows Rembrandt's desire, after his enthusiastic and prolific youth, to radically rework his painting, in the light of his later painterly vision. This is no slow evolution of his art, as was the case with *The Night Watch*, completed in 1642 after several years' work; this is a radical revision of a painting which had been completed many years previously, transforming it into a completely new work, produced using a different technique designed with a new sensitivity. *Danae* thus summarises the two stages of his artistic life without the result being hybrid and denatured.

During the 1640s, Rembrandt painted many portrait. The diversity of his approach and the variety of brushstrokes gave them considerable importance. The simplicity and modesty of the portraiture caused great admiration and is indicative of the painter's talent and maturity.

The *Portrait of Baartjen Doomer* (1640) and the *Portrait of an Old Woman* (1650) – exhibited respectively at the Hermitage Museum in St Petersburg and the Fine Arts Museum in Moscow – mark the beginning of the end of the artist's studies in this field. This was an unhappy period in the artist's private life.

In 1639, while his contemporaries were celebrating his genius, Rembrandt and his wife moved to the house he had just bought for thirteen thousand florins in the Jodenbreestraat, in Amsterdam. It was an elegant bourgeois dwelling on three floors, embellished with sculptures, and which inspired great pride in him until it precipitated him into financial difficulties.

His lifestyle was important to him, but he was also one of the most handsomely rewarded painters in Holland. He could easily command one hundred florins for a portrait, while the paintings of most of his contemporaries would be lucky to get between twelve and seventy-five florins. Fortune smiled on him until the death of his mother in 1640, and Saskia's demise two years later put an end to his joie de vivre. His son, Titus, born in 1641, would be his comfort and support until he died in 1668, six months before the birth of his daughter.

19. *Saskia van Uylenburgh in Arcadian Costume*, 1635. Oil on canvas, 123.5 x 97.5 cm. The National Gallery, London.

During this period, Holland became very wealthy as a result of its great maritime adventures, and was now becoming settled and complacent, confident in its future, and started to seek refuge in the conformity of its Golden Age and began to reject some of the great artists who had previously been highly acclaimed. This was the fate of Franz Hals, who was now supplanted by painters with a greater aristocratic refinement, such as Gerard Dou, Ferdinand Bol and Govaert Flinck, all of whom had studied under Rembrandt.

The paintings in the Russian museums perfectly illustrate the tone which the artist gave his portraits during this decade. Baartjen Maertens Doomer, whom he portrayed in 1640, was not in high society, she was the wife of a craftsman who had close contacts in artistic circles; Rembrandt was immune to the conventions and he created this portrait with complete freedom, following his artistic impulses. He reproduces the lively expression of the lady whose cheerfulness emerges in every stroke. The whole depiction is based on the drawing which Rembrandt created as an integral part of the painting, following the expression to become more and more precise as the painting took shape. Painting his sitters as they really were, he imbued the portraits with their whole personality in order the better to bring them to life.

In seeking to bring out the "mobility" of the sitters, Rembrandt managed to obtain a likeness such as no one had ever been able to achieve hitherto. For more than ten years this method led to the apotheosis of Rembrandt's work.

The *Portrait of an Old Woman*, painted in 1650, was in the same vein. With complete mastery of his art, he gradually eradicated the dual perception of the world which had prevailed in his work hitherto, and which was typical of the previous decade, which consisted in distinguishing commissioned work from his personal vision of art, separating historical panels from the portraits. These works would now be combined in a single vision of the world which now bore a single signature – that of Rembrandt. The large red cloth in *The Old Woman*, which was by no means typical of the time but which was favoured by the Master, as well as the old-fashioned "Burgundian" dress give the feeling that this was not so much a commissioned painting but rather a work of the artist's own inspiration. Yet the method used and the strict "objectivity" of the portrait are reminders that at the time Rembrandt had gained complete artistic freedom which would never be diminished.

20. *The Incredulity of St Thomas*, 1634. Oil on wood (oak), 50 x 51 cm. The Pushkin Museum of Fine Arts, Moscow.

"Man and his state of mind" would become one of his major interests, and the older he became, the more he reflected upon the internal solitude of those whose portraits he painted, in his eyes the only vector of a meticulous transcription of the personality, which through experience and observation he was able to turn into flesh and blood. By fixing a moment of life on the canvas without ever stopping it in its course, he was able to portray the richness hidden within his models and to make a look, an expression betray their most intimate thoughts and the secret of their existence.

Even those portraits which were his personal inspiration, for which Rembrandt often used the same models over and over, express the diverse nature of the "soul" and the profound nature of the human beings whom he placed within his genre scenes. That is how he "unmasked" his older brother, Adriaen van Rijn, whose features were used as a medium for characterisation in the various portraits of old men painted in the 1650s. These paintings are of great interest to those wishing to study the "Rembrandt method".

The two *Portrait of an Old Lady* painted in 1654, in the Hermitage Museum in St Petersburg and the Pushkin Museum in Moscow, used the same model and respond to the same criteria as regards their creation. The technique adopted, which is unique to the artist, is very varied as regards the manner of applying the colours around the eyes and in the shaded parts of the face. It is a series of brushstrokes and semi-transparent patches of colour whose outlines are blurred.

There are areas which are brightly lit, and a heavy layer of impasto consisting of short and long strokes of different colours. This method enables the artist to pass from light to dark, a technique he mastered better than anyone. Finally, over and above the intelligent amalgam of colours, the position occupied by these brushstrokes in space and the direction of the paintbrush on the canvas contribute to the three-dimensional effect so often admired in Rembrandt's work. There are numerous variations on these techniques among a number of Dutch artists, but theirs never matches the sureness with which Rembrandt used them.

In Rembrandt, the human face was always associated with the life which had shaped it. Furthermore, each portrait reflected a particular attitude in which the enigmas of existence could be read. The elderly people he painted in 1654 had a particularly

21. *Christ Revealing Himself to the Emmaüs' Pilgrims*, 1648. Oil on canvas, 68 x 65 cm. Musée du Louvre, Paris.

tragic view of the world. They knew life to be full of pain, injustice and cruelty. This world view was familiar to them, however, and did not cause them to rebel against it within themselves. Their loneliness was manifest, but it did not prevent the artist from discovering the complex ties which bound them to life, which he revealed in their wrinkled faces.

Rembrandt's old people are the incarnation of human wisdom. An exceptional spiritual value places these individuals above the daily routine and confers a tragic grandeur upon them and converts their philosophy into an absolute truth, one worthy of the whole nation. These portraits mark the apogee of seventeenth-century art in Europe, and have no direct descendants. It was not until two centuries later that artists would once again tackle the ambiguous relationship between man and his soul; but in the works of the romantic painters, the common people were not considered to have the wisdom or the grandeur of the figures painted by Rembrandt. His genius was to place them in a setting which would best express their personalities, so that in their individual expression they would lose any disadvantage conferred by their social status.

Rembrandt transferred his own feelings to his model. Having found in a human being what he shared with them in terms of their view of the world and their state of mind, he painted each of the numerous portraits which made him famous like a fresco reflecting the image of his century. Less than a genre, Rembrandt's portrait is scrap of truth torn from mankind.

Despite the importance of landscape painting and genre scenes, the Dutch painters continued to draw their inspiration for subject-matter from portraiture. Since such portraits were a source of both honour and profit, many artists were unable to resist flattering the images commissioned by their patrons and this has not always contributed to the posthumous reputation of the artists. Seeking to please rather than to "bring out the expression", many of Rembrandt's pupils abandoned the style which best suited them, large brushstrokes and thick paint for a lighter touch, one which was smooth and too frequently inconsequential. This was a style which many used, born of financial success the growth of the middle classes and changes in fashion.

Even though the most competent painters translated this shift of opinion, which was already being served by such masters as van Dyck, Rembrandt did not become one of

22. *The Descent from the Cross*, 1634. Oil on canvas, 158 x 117 cm. The State Hermitage Museum, St Petersburg.

23. *The Conspiracy of the Batavians under Claudius Civilis*, c. 1666. Oil on canvas, 196 x 309 cm. Nationalmuseum, Stockholm.

them and continued to defy the artistic currents and his accumulating financial woes working without making the slightest concession to fashion. In the late 1640s, when Hendrickje Stoffels, became his model and went to live with him in the house on Jodenbreestraat, he continued to pursue his own aesthetic style, alternating commissioned portraits with those of his own inspiration, and with historical scenes in which he adroitly combined his models with his own "visions" of the world.

24. *The Deposition*, 1633. Oil on panel, 89.4 x 65,2 cm. Alte Pinakothek, Munich.

His artistic language had attained an unequalled virtuosity. Sometimes resorting to very simple methods, sometimes using an ingenious and complex mixture of brushstrokes (thick, semi-transparent or transparent), he managed to create "unities of the soul" in which each element is inseparable from the whole. There is

25. *Abraham's Sacrifice*,
    c. 1636. Drawing.
    The British Museum,
    London.

26. *Abraham's Sacrifice*, 1635.
    Oil on canvas,
    193 x 132.5 cm.
    The State Hermitage
    Museum, St Petersburg.

no splash of colour, no brushstroke which is not important in itself, all the elements of the artistic language have acquired a psychological and spiritual basis which only exists to the extent that they are imbued with it. That is why it is practically impossible to extract and isolate the image from its psychology and to find adequate terminology with which to define it. It is an element which is inherent in painting.

In the second half of the 17th century, Holland was to experience a series of upheavals, such as the war against England in 1652. This was the start of a difficult period.

At this time, while the Dutch were fearful of their future, Rembrandt, like a magician who remains untouched by current events, continued to present the public with images of a different reality. Deaf to the agitation of the Dutch populace, he lived in a world which he had redrawn to his own specifications, consisting of reds, browns and blacks, whites and yellows mixed in subtle touches, melting together on the canvas beneath his magical brushes.

He seemed to care only about his combinations of colour and light with which he played so skillfully in the midst of the shadows. Rembrandt was so captivated by his art, it became almost an obsession, and he could only perceive the world through his paintings. Pursuing his dream, brushes in hand, he continued to create portraits in oils and to make etchings of others, yet without abandoning the scenes from the Bible in which people and the world were reflected.

Life continued around him but he appeared to remain unaware of it. He embarked upon a tumultuous course which led him into the greatest financial difficulties. The artist had been showered with honours and the love of Hendrickje, the patient force behind his illuminations, had hidden the serious consequences and had detached him from the conventional and pompous society with which he refused to compromise.

In July, 1656, heavily in debt, Rembrandt found himself unable to meet his commitments. His income no longer covered his expenditure and he was forced to leave his lovely home in Amsterdam, abandoning it to the bailiffs. His magnificent art collection, which included many contemporary works, as well as those by Raphael, Giorgione and van Eyck, antique statues and Chinese and Japanese works of art, suits of armour, minerals and even a lion skin, was auctioned off. Yet he was not driven into bankruptcy.

Hendrickje and her son Titus turned themselves into a firm of art dealers and made the Master into their employee, so that the income from the sale of his pictures would not be swallowed up in reimbursements to his creditors.

Rembrandt's new home in the working-class Rosengracht district, was by no means unpleasant. He continued to work ceaselessly despite adversity, drawing inspiration from the working people though still retaining the friendship, and even the admiration, of the great and the good. In 1667, Cosimo de Medici, the future Grand

27. *The Parable of the Labourers in the Vineyard*, 1637. Oil on wood panel (oak), 31 x 42 cm. The State Hermitage Museum, St Petersburg.

28. *Herman Doomer (born about 1595, died 1650)*, 1640. Oil on wood, 75.2 x 55.2 cm. The Metropolitan Museum of Art, H. O. Havemeyer Collection, New York.

29. *Portrait of Baertje Martens*, c. 1640. Oil on wood panel (oak), 76 x 56 cm. The State Hermitage Museum, St Petersburg.

Duke of Tuscany, visited him in his studio in order to purchase one of the two *Self-Portrait* which are now in the Uffizi Gallery, in Florence.

While measuring the inanity of human pretentions, Rembrandt was able to escape the self-pity of deep depression because even in this time of crisis, he still had his painting left. His work lost more constraints and became more ethereal.

The 1650s produced more master-pieces in the painter's catalogue, some of which are in the Russian Museums. The *Young Woman Trying on Earrings* dates from 1657. It is a painting of a rather rare type in which a young beauty admires herself in a mirror. Although this is an allegorical image of vanity which was very much of the period,

30. *Return of the Prodigal Son.* Drawing. Teyler Museum, Haarlem.

31. *David and Jonathan,* 1642. Oil on wood panel (oak), 73 x 61.5 cm. The State Hermitage Museum, St Petersburg.

it cannot rival *The Return of the Prodigal Son,* generally considered to be the perfect illustration of Rembrandt's mature genius. The latter painting gives a good idea of the artist's own philosophy of life, and his attitude towards existence, which he regarded as artificial and superfluous.

The historical paintings of the last decade of his life clearly illustrate the essence of Rembrandt's art, the subjects which interested him the most and what he was able to offer in terms of aesthetics.

Haman, Esther and Ahasuerus, painted in 1660, is indisputably one of the most peaceful paintings of the Master, as well as one of the most taciturn. Esther has just made her accusation to the king who sinks into a profound meditation, refusing to believe the truth revealed to him. The lack of any outside action and the apparent isolation of the figures from each other enables the artist to reveal the character of each of them, the relationship between them and the fate that awaits them.

Man face-to-face with himself: this was Rembrandt's major preoccupation when he painted a portrait. It was these same problems, seen from another era, transposed to the biblical world, which would continue to preoccupy him until he breathed his last.

Each of the figures in *Haman Recognizes His Fate* (1665) painted in the foreground against a dark background, seems to be searching his own soul; although there is no explicit indication which would interpret the scene exactly, the relationship between the protagonists clearly illustrates the painter's intentions. An oriental dignitary accepts his loss and accepts his fate with self-denial and a monarch who has just ordered his arrest and execution, yet whose face expresses sadness rather than his wrath. An old man and several prophets are witnesses to the scene.

Yet it is in *the Return of the Prodigal Son* painted in 1668-1669, that Rembrandt attained the perfection of his art. It was a historical quest which had reached its conclusion, the Gospel parable made flesh and for the artist perhaps, who was over sixty when he painted it, though in a perpetual quest for the truth, a response to the preplexing question of the supreme meaning of life. The reuniting of father and son were a possible summing up of their earthly existence and all the sufferings experienced during their long separation. Man is shaped by his own past. The moment of the actual meeting is so emotional that legitimate joy has given way to something resembling sadness, but which is probably more like a serene melancholy, regret for the lost years.

Although very different as to the dates when they were painted, the scale of the figures, the size of the canvas, the composition and even the technique give these three works perfect spiritual unity through the emotions they portray. It has been said that the heroes in Rembrandt's later works exist "outside time and space".

32. *Old Woman with Glasses*, 1643.
Oil on wood,
61 x 49 cm.
The State Hermitage Museum, St Petersburg.

This is only true if one considers that they exist outside a space filled with everyday objects and that they live outside time filled with everyday routine.

Their lives are governed by a clock which does not apply here on earth, it is a different rhythm of time and space. There had been a period when the artist had delighted in creating an imaginary and flamboyant Orient. Henceforward this type of background seemed to him to be superfluous and he contented himself with dressing his figures in a few exotic fripperies. All other indications of place and time are absent or merely hinted at. The Roman portico in the *Prodigal Son* is barely discernible, the table, the ewer, the dish of apples and the cup in Human's hand are the only indications of the feast held by Esther and Ahasuerus. In *the Return of the Prodigal Son*, the artist went as

33. *The Prophetess Anna* (known as *Rembrandt's Mother*), 1631. Oil on panel, 60 x 48 cm. Rijksmuseum, Amsterdam.

34. Drawing from Raphael's *Portrait of Baldassare Castiglione*. Albertina, Vienna.

far as leaving out the characters mentioned in the Bible and who had been part of the pictorial tradition of the parable.

In Rembrandt's works created in the 1630s, the importance of the action was determined by the magnificent backgrounds. Those of the 1640s were characterised by their depictions of everyday scenes.

Henceforward, as his final works show, everything concentrated on the inner worlds of the figures whose intensity throws back into the shade anything that appears to be subordinate. The painter now concentrates completely on the soul of his models and

35. *Portrait of an Old Man.*
Oil on wood panel
(oak), 51 x 42 cm.
The State Hermitage
Museum, St Petersburg.

36. *Child in a Cradle,*
c. 1645. Drawing.
Unknown location.

37. *The Holy Family*, 1645.
Oil on canvas,
117 x 91 cm.
The State Hermitage
Museum, St Petersburg.

38. *Danae*, 1636.
Oil on canvas, 185 x 202.5 cm.
The State Hermitage Museum,
St Petersburg.

39. *The Holy Family* also
    known as *The Carpenter's*
    Family (detail), 1640.
    Oil on wood panel,
    41 x 34 cm.
    Musée du Louvre, Paris.

40. *Old Man in an Armchair*,
   1652.
   Oil on canvas,
   111 x 88 cm.
   The National Gallery,
   London.

41. *Portrait of an Old Lady*,
   1654. Oil on canvas,
   82 x 72 cm.
   The Pushkin Museum
   of Fine Arts, Moscow.

42. *Portrait of an Old Man in Red*, 1652-1654. Oil on canvas, 108 x 86 cm. The State Hermitage Museum, St Petersburg.

43. *Portrait of an Old Jew,*
1654. Oil on canvas,
109 x 85 cm.
The State Hermitage
Museum, St Petersburg.

44. *Old Lady Reading*, 1655.
Duke of Buccleuch's
Collection, Scotland.

45. *Portrait of an Old Lady*,
1654. Oil on canvas,
109 x 84 cm.
The State Hermitage
Museum, St Petersburg.

has deep compassion for them. They are looking inwards at themselves, and all the attention is focused upon them. Everything that is secondary and fortuitous is eliminated in order to show what is in their minds.

Rembrandt's figures are now either immersed in the limelight or almost invisibly submerged in shadows, depending on the painter's whim. Yet wherever they are placed in the painting, they remain isolated from the world and from other human beings, as if strangers to the course of life. One sometimes has the impression that they cannot see, despite the ties which bind them to their common fate.

Rembrandt's figures passively accept the grand designs which are their inexorable fate but they are also confronted with their own lives. Even Esther, who by her actions directed the course of events in order to deliver her people from a hideous fate, is eventually merely an instrument of God's will and that of Mordecai. The beautiful gentle queen performs what is written for all eternity with a dignity that is full of modesty. In Rembrandt's later work, human life is attached to the concept of destiny which while being inherent in man, escapes him completely. His destiny can be followed with dignity, the figures seem to say to the Old Master, one may rebel internally but it is not possible to fight it.

Rembrandt's sombre genius understood the sad, almost unconscious undertone of this impassioned impetus. There is an echo here of everything that would be most surprising in the work of Byron. "Before me there is the head of a man who with one clean line can only be half-seen", wrote the young poet Lermontov two hundred years later when viewing a Rembrandt's portrait. "All around, there are only shadows. His haughty expression is both burning and yet at the same time full of anguish and doubt. Perhaps you have painted it from nature, and that this effigy is far from being ideal! Perhaps you have depicted yourself as you were during your years of suffering? Yet a cold look could never penetrate this great mystery and this extraordinary work will remain a bitter reproach to heartless people".

46. *Portrait of an Old Lady*, 1654. Oil on canvas, 74 x 63 cm. The Pushkin Museum of Fine Arts, Moscow.

The character of Rembrandt's figures are deaf to this vision of man which the Romantic period would celebrate with such misguided enthusiasm. It is probably *Titus van Rijn in a Monk's Habit* which Lermontov, then only 16 years old, described in his poem about a Rembrandt painting. This work was then in the collection of the Counts Stroganov in St Petersburg and the young man was suddenly inspired and saw the

47. *Portrait of Adriaen
    van Rijn*, 1654.
    Oil on canvas,
    74 x 63 cm.
    The Pushkin Museum
    of Fine Arts, Moscow.

48. *Self-Portrait*, 1652.
    Oil on canvas,
    112 x 61.5 cm.
    Kunsthistorisches
    Museum, Vienna.

49. *Saskia (?) in Front of
a Mirror*, c. 1630.
Drawing. Musées
royaux des Beaux-Arts
de Belgique, Brussels.

50. *Young Lady Trying On
Earrings*, 1657.
Oil on wood panel,
39.5 x 32.5 cm.
The State Hermitage
Museum, St Petersburg.

image of the heroes who populated his own world and his imagination. In his eyes, this painting is an incarnation of "the great mystery of art" and the even more inaccessible mystery of his own destiny. The poet describes the "sombre genius" of the painter and identifies with the passion and sufferings of the artist and his loneliness in the world.

The artist's philosophy, his subjective vision of the world are those of a convinced sceptic. The tragedy inherent in Rembrandt's last paintings is generally explained by the adversity he had suffered, and the painful solitude he had experienced as an artist.

Saskia's death and the subsequent death of Titus in 1668 certainly affected him deeply since he was very sensitive and all that he felt in his heart is reflected in the faces of his figures. The economic crisis in the Low Countries, as well as his own financial difficulties also decisively affected his work. Yet it was not so much the outside influences as his own innermost nature which he was painting in the shadow and light of his good and bad days. In Rembrandt, even happiness had its own colour but it was the colour of melancholy. Even the two women who had done something to brighten his son's existence after Saskia's death – Hendrickje Stoffels from 1649 until her death in 1663, then Magdalen van Loo after 1668 – did nothing to change his vision of mankind. There is evidence of its in his early work, and his later works only reinforced his attitude.

Rembrandt Harmen Gerritszoon van Rijn died on 4 October, 1669, leaving more than six hundred paintings and an impressive series of etchings. There were portraits, religious subjects, landscapes and genre scenes. The paintings which can be seen in the Russian museums give a clear idea of his art because the collection summarises his life's work and the manner in which it evolved. The portraits show the brilliance of his art and the variety of subject-matter in his historic paintings show the diversity of approach.

Rembrandt's work, which is so strongly personal, occupies a unique place not only in painting but in the whole of European culture. When Rembrandt is compared with his predecessors or even with his successors, one can see the total originality of his creativity and can precisely measure the place he occupies in our spiritual heritage. Tsar Peter the Great brought the first Rembrandt's to Russia. He first had the idea in 1697 during his first trip abroad. Yuri Kologrivov visited The Hague in 1715 and returned with 43 paintings to be used to adorn the Palace of Montplaisir at Peterhof, which was then still under construction. But his task was not complete, since he then travelled successively to Antwerp and Brussels, finally acquiring 117 other paintings by Amsterdam's Old Master. At the same time, the ambassador Kuranin and commercial attaché Soloviov were entrusted with a similar mission. The result was that in the following year, 150 paintings entered the Russian collections. This was a period during which Rembrandt's paintings were considered to be either "heretical" or old-fashioned. They rarely came up for public auction and when they did so they fetched derisory sums. The first paintings were hung in the Hermitage in 1764, less than 100 years after the artist's death. They represented a lot of 225 paintings, consigned by a merchant from Berlin as part-payment of a debt which he owned to the Imperial treasury.

51. *Bathsheba at Her Bath*, 1654. Oil on canvas, 141 x 141 cm. Musée du Louvre, Paris.

Prince Golytsin, the charge d'affaires in Paris, and a friend of Diderot and Falconet, also played a very active part in the adornment of the new art gallery. Two major works now in the Hermitage owe their presence to his endeavours. These are *Portrait of An Old Woman in Spectacles* and *The Return of the Prodigal Son*. In St Petersburg, Rembrandt continued to enjoy a high reputation. The Imperial Russian court showed great enthusiasm for the work of the Dutch Master who had no equal in western Europe where his works continued to be regarded at best with indifference, at worst with disdain. For instance, in 1772 Falconet wrote as follows to Catherine II: "I received notice from France that there is a perfectly beautiful Rembrandt painting

52. *Hendrickje Stoffels*, c. 1652.
Oil on canvas, 74 x 61 cm.
Musée du Louvre, Paris.

53. *Christ and the Woman of Samaria*, 1658. Etching.

54. *Christ and the Woman
of Samaria*, 1659.
Oil on canvas,
60 x 75 cm.
The State Hermitage
Museum, St Petersburg.

55. *Haman, Esther and
Ahasuerus*, 1660.
Oil on canvas,
73 x 94 cm.
The Pushkin Museum
of Fine Arts, Moscow.

56. *Portrait of a Man*,
    1661. Oil on canvas,
    71 x 61 cm.
    The State Hermitage
    Museum, St Petersburg.

57. *Aristotle with a Bust*
    of Homer, 1653.
    Oil on canvas,
    143.5 x 136.5 cm.
    The Metropolitan
    Museum of Art,
    New York.

58. *The Return of the*
    Prodigal Son, c. 1668.
    Oil on canvas,
    262 x 205 cm.
    The State Hermitage
    Museum, St Petersburg.

59. *Haman Recognizes
His Fate*, c. 1665.
Oil on canvas,
127 x 116 cm.
The State Hermitage
Museum, St Petersburg.

available which makes a pair with the *Prodigal Son*. If it really is as good as that, then this item would be worthy of your gallery. If your Imperial Majesty should command me to do so, I shall write to one of our best artists to go and see the painting and to judge whether it is as good as it is reported to be; because I am very wary of giving this task to any others. The subject is Mordecai at the feet of Esther and Ahasuerus. The price is three thousand six hundred pounds". Shortly thereafter, Catherine replied to Falconnet that if the painting was as good as her *Prodigal Son* she would be happy to pay that price. In fact, the sale never proceeded, although the painting remained in Paris for 15 years without finding a purchaser. Today it adorns the walls of the

Bucharest Museum. In 1769, after several years of legal battles, the collection of Count Heinrich Brühl, former minister of Augustus III of Saxony, was acquired by the Hermitage. Among the treasures amassed by the count and his secretary, who was the curator of the Print Room of Dresden and an informed art critic, there were four Rembrandts, *Portrait of an Old Man* and *Portrait of an Old Man in Red* now in St Petersburg, as well as *Portrait of Adriaen van Rijn* and *Portrait of an Old Woman* which are now in the Pushkin Museum in Moscow. *David and Uriah, Flora, Danae* and *The Sacrifice of Abraham* are among numerous acquisitions made throughout the 18th century, after the deaths of many great foreign collectors.

61. *Sampling Officials of the Drapers' Guild*, 1662. Oil on canvas, 191.5 x 279 cm. Rijksmuseum, Amsterdam.

LIST OF ILLUSTRATIONS